An Illinois Boyhood

CARL VAN DOREN

NEW YORK

The Viking Press

1939

An Illinois Boyhood

I WAS born in a village then called Hope, in Illinois, and I lived there or on a farm a mile away till I was fifteen, as happy as an animal. After we had decided to leave the village for a town, I was suddenly restless. Through four or five dragging months I blamed the farm and the village, though they were the same as they had been. I resented country manners, country clothes, country grammar. Ambition in me first took the form of snobbishness. I believe this is more general than many people will confess.

My brothers were too young to have clear opinions on the change, and my father and mother had simple motives. Living in town would be easier than in the country, and there would be better schools for the boys. But all of us, whether aware of it or not, were in the drift of an impulse which in 1900 was common in Illinois and throughout the Middle West. Farming had become old-fashioned. The successful farmers were retiring, as they called it, to the towns, leaving their farms to be rented by the less successful or to be run by hired labor. The value of land, at least the price, had risen so fast in a generation that the owners had turned from working farmers into landlords. Few of them looked farther than to the county seat, or even to the nearest railroad station, but they did look and they did move from the land. It was a powerful instinctive migration which was to transform a large part of America.

When I call Hope a village I use a word for it which nobody there ever used. Hope was a church, a school, a blacksmith shop, one store at first and two after a while, and ten houses, in which, in fifteen years, not more than fifty persons lived. It lay at a cross-roads on the long slope of a terminal moraine in the middle of a prairie. The horizon was a circle on the plain, and the sky bent down and met it in a level line. The sun came up out of Indiana as if it were the ocean. The sunsets were sky-high and horizon-wide and rainbow-colored. The soil underfoot was as black as the nights, springing up annually into lavish corn and oats and hay, and some wheat, and along the roads and hedges into a tumult of weeds. In the hot summers they said you could hear the corn grow.

Corn pressed in on Hope like a tame jungle. The site of the village had been cut out of two farms which surrounded it. Behind them were others which belonged hardly less to the village than the houses in it. Most of the men saw each other almost every day at the store or the blacksmith shop. The children went five days of the week during nine months of the year to school. And everybody met everybody else at church on Sunday. Although the village was a bare cross-roads in a cornfield, it was also the heart of a community, with the bones, flesh, blood, and nerves of any community. Any community is a world.

2

HOPE had theology and religion. The church belonged to one of the small sects which are the fringes of Protestantism. I never heard the name of it till I was grown. The preacher did not live at Hope but came Saturday, preached morning and evening on Sunday, and left on Monday, the guest in turn of various households of the congregation. It cannot have been easy for him to satisfy his audiences. There were still in Hope a few hardshell and hellfire pioneers who wanted sterner doctrine than they got from the sermons. There was a family of skeptics, a man and his sons, who came occasionally to church and were believed to be listening with secret sneers. There was a family of Quakers. There were unregenerate sinners, husbands of pious wives, who behaved well enough in church but who had never joined it. And on Sunday there was always half a churchful of sleepy children who wished they could go outdoors and play.

The church at Hope was a sober club for the encouragement of good behavior. While a few members were devout or dogmatic, most of them were easy-going in whatever faith they had. The motto painted in bold letters on the wall behind the pulpit, Christian Character the Test of Fellowship, made up the whole creed. To be honest and decent in daily affairs was all that was required of any member, and that was required rather by the community than by the church alone. At the annual revivals new members joined the church, most of them children who had come to adolescence the past year. But I never saw anything like a religious orgy at Hope. Such uproar went with camp-meetings in backward villages. Nor did the support of the church put burdens on the congregation, which paid what it chose to afford. The people of Hope were not like the Germans to the west, who, Hope believed, would let the minister get them into the church, lock the door, and tell them how much money they must raise before they could go about their usual business.

And yet the church meant more to Hope than any club. It had a kind of music that wound itself into the memory. Not the wheezing cottage organ. Not the dry hymns. Not the drone of the preacher. But the music of rich, proud words from the Bible falling upon ears that had heard them again and again and now heard them chime with old recollections. The silence during prayer. The hush at communion. All sorts of thoughts and feelings, of course, ran through the passive minds of the worshipers: vows, fears, loves, hates, lusts, resentments, repentances, forecasts, griefs, triumphs. But they had in common one strain of piety, a sense of reverence toward a ceremonial which had become a part of them, reaching back to their childhood, and bringing them at each repetition the accumulated experience of solemn hours. This piety was Hope's religion.

Sunday school was livelier. Every Sunday there was a passage of Scripture to be studied, with such comments as the teachers knew how to make, and a Golden Text to be memorized. After an opening hymn and a prayer, the classes scattered to various parts of the church's one room, the most envied class to the gallery. Nobody took much interest in the day's lesson, except to see what picture would be on the card which every child was given to help him remember the passage he was supposed to have read. When the school had reassembled it was exciting to watch one of the teachers write on a blackboard the numbers of those present in the classes and of the pennies they had contributed.

What we learned out of the Old and New Testaments stayed in us by the most unconscious assimilation. Yet I cannot now read any part of the Bible without remembering as much as reading. My memory runs just ahead of my eyes, and I catch up with it like a man visiting the house where he lived as a child.

It may be because I was so young that my mind seldom went beyond Hope in thinking about church and Sunday school, but I doubt that in this I was different from my elders. For these modes of worship had not been imposed by any alien sovereign hierarchy to which the congregation was subject. Hope had itself imported them to meet its own needs.

About the time of the Civil War, when the township had been settled only a few years, my Grandfather Butz came home one evening to find his wife gone from the house. A little later she returned, on horseback. A tall girl, already gaunt from hard work and prairie weather, she got down from her horse and faced her husband with flushed cheeks but determined eyes.

"Where in the nation have you been?" My grandfather was a Whig and a conservative.

My grandmother was a Republican and a radical. "I have been around to the neighbors to ask them to come to Sunday school next Sunday."

"What Sunday school?" Hope had then no church and nothing but a temporary schoolhouse a muddy mile away from the cross-roads.

"We're going to organize a Sunday school. I'm tired of having the men waste all their Sundays on horse races. It's a bad example for the children. Next Sunday everybody has promised to meet at the schoolhouse."

This was a long speech from my grandmother, and it was probably all she said while my grandfather objected and debated, and finally agreed and admired. On Sunday they drove, in a farm wagon for want of any other vehicle, to what was to be Sunday school.

The schoolhouse sat naked on the prairie. The first man who came tied his team to the hitching-post in front. The next one tied his to the rear wheels of the first wagon. And so on in a straggling, stamping line. The women and children went inside as soon as they arrived. The men stood outside, talking about everything but what had brought them there. Time passed with nothing done because nobody knew what to do.

My grandfather was not a patient man. "Men," he said, "we came here to organize a Sunday school. Suppose we go in and get it started." They filed in and sat down on the hard benches.

Another silence. More impatience from my grandfather, who had a tongue. He rose and called the meeting to order.

"Ladies and gentlemen, we have met to organize a Sunday school. I don't know much about Sunday schools, but I think the first thing is to elect a superintendent. Do I hear any nominations?"

There was a buzzing on the benches. Someone nominated my grandmother. There were no other nominations. My grandmother was elected. She was too shy to stand up and say a word that day. Someone thought they should have an assistant superintendent. My grandfather was nominated and elected.

With that the meeting halted. They all felt there should be

some kind of prayer, but there was not a "praying man" in the house. They gave that up. Two or three of those present remembered a Sunday school hymn they had heard. They taught the others. The opening verse ran:

> The Sunday school, that blessed place!
>   Oh, I had rather stay
> Within its walls, a child of grace,
>   Than spend my hours at play.

They sang the verse several times, and perhaps other verses. It was the only hymn, and the only music, they had for weeks to follow.

The next Sunday Uncle Tom Snyder, a praying man and an ordained occasional preacher, came and helped them through the service. My grandmother took her horse again and rode among the neighbors till she collected seven dollars to send to Cincinnati for printed weekly lessons. After that the Sunday school was never interrupted. Hope's form of spiritual life had been set up.

A better schoolhouse was built on an acre of ground which my grandfather gave out of his farm at the cross-roads. Taxes paid for it. Voluntary pockets built a church. Though there was talk of uniting with the Methodists, the congregation chose the New Lights instead. Possibly they thought the Methodist doctrine and discipline too strict or too explicit. More likely their choice was on the whole an accident. In any case, Hope in its own way made up its own mind. It had taken its first step when it undertook to civilize its Sundays, much as it might have undertaken to improve its bridges. Church and preachers came as a natural next step. The order of worship might be imported, but the motive to import one had been native, and native motives established and continued it.

The earliest preachers, two or three of whom survived to years which I can remember, were bearded, ignorant, honest men who farmed during the week and on Sunday preached loud sermons against the grosser faults of the community. Such preachers satisfied their generation. The sons and daughters of that generation looked upon them as relics of the pioneer time, which was so recent but seemed so remote. The later preachers shaved their faces and were softer, like the new generation. The church kept pace with its world. In 1860 Hope was open prairie. In 1885, when I was born, the community was as settled in its virtues and vices as if it had been there a thousand years.

3

THESE years saw a change in the school at Hope. The earliest memory of which I can fix the date takes me back to a September day when I stood at the fence of our house in the village and watched the children playing in the schoolyard next door. I was four that day, and I boasted of it to some of them who spoke to me as they ran by. But what I remember best is seeing the teacher limp across the yard from his house just behind it. I was afraid of him, a sour, savage man who, I now know, had taught there so long that he was tolerated but had come to be disapproved. He died soon after. I have no other memories of him and no knowledge but what I gathered from the legend which outlasted him.

On the day of his marriage, one of my great-aunts told me, he left the wedding party to sit behind the stove and study an arithmetic book. My father told me the teacher had formerly believed that Chinese eyes do not move in their sockets —he had read that the Chinese have "oblique-set" eyes! My mother told me that when she was five or six the teacher had terrified her by making her sit, as punishment for some little failure, on the floor and put her finger through a knot-hole, telling her that if she were not a better girl a dreadful beast might bite her finger off. Against his cruelty, my grandmother told me, there had been a rebellion in the school itself. Once, when he had said that the next day he was going to whip some of the big girls, my mother now among them, the bigger boys, including my uncles, met after school and swore they would not permit it. They were going to bring a rope to school and, if he tried to carry out his threat, tie him up and beat him. An older man overheard, told one or two others, and warned the teacher. Knowing him and the boys, they were afraid that in the fight which was sure to take place someone might be hurt or even killed. This was mutiny, as surely as if the school had been a ship. Whatever fury the teacher may have felt, the big girls were not punished, and the affair was dropped without a word. The community knew how to look out for itself better than how to talk about it.

The good things said of the tyrant were that he kept order among the rowdiest boys who came to school only in the winter, that he drilled the elements of learning unforgettably into his pupils, and that he grounded them once for all in the distinction between right and wrong. But he passed with the old days and the old need for his kind, if there ever had been such a need. My first teacher, shortly after his death, was a young girl, and no child thought of disobeying her. The pioneer school survived only in the pioneer teacher. When he was gone, it was gone.

I did not start to school till my brother Guy, two years younger, was old enough to go with me. By that time we had moved from the village to a farm, and for the next six years we walked a mile back and forth on every school day from the first of September to the first of June. There were days enough when we had to stagger through snowdrifts or pick our way among puddles of black mud, but I remember best the mornings in late April or early May when we were allowed to begin going barefoot. As our father was the doctor, our appearance without shoes was a prescription to the other children. Many shoes and stockings came off on those mornings, and many feet, blanched and softened since October, ran wild in a happy, wincing freedom.

All the school days of the six years seem now to have been alike. From nine to twelve, with fifteen minutes' recess, we sat at hard double desks and benches without moving or speaking except when we went forward to recite. The children who lived in the village had to go home to dinner. The rest of us raced for our dinner-pails, waiting on shelves at the back of the room, and, again in our seats, raced to see who could first be done with his hearty sandwiches, hardboiled eggs, pie or cake, and possibly milk carried in the hollow lid of the dinner-pail. Nobody went hungry and nobody was hurt by eating too fast. There was some trading in food, but most of us ate what we brought. At least once every day some boy cracked an egg shell on another boy's head. But the real business of the noon hour was not eating. In fifteen minutes we were playing rounders, or handy-over, or dare base, or I spy. In winter we built snow forts and defended and assaulted them, or went skating on the brook—called the branch—which ran just east of the village. Once when we were skating we did not hear the bell, or by a sly conspiracy refused to hear it, and had to stay in after school for three days to make up the time lost. On every other day for six years the bell at one o'clock brought us in to another three hours divided and spent like the three hours in the forenoon.

Our schooling was plain fare. Outside of a little singing and drawing and book-keeping, we gave our whole time to reading, grammar, writing, spelling, arithmetic, geography, physiology, and American history. So far as we were ever taught, the human race had had a past in only two parts of the world: in Judea, which we learned about on Sundays, and in America, during the week. The human body in our physiology had no means of reproducing itself and no impulse to do it. We did not mind. We had watched the animals and discussed our elders. Geography was maps and boundaries, capitals and principal products. When later I first saw mountains I was surprised that they were not tidy cones, as in the pictures I had seen in school.

Arithmetic came nearer home. We learned how to measure land in square rods and acres and square miles: always square measures for square land, such as we knew. Forty acres were an exact square a quarter of a mile each way, and a day's work with a cultivator in a cornfield, ten acres or a hundred rows, was a walk of twenty-five miles. We learned how many pounds make a bushel of corn in the ear, of shelled corn, oats, wheat, rye, potatoes, and how many bushels would fill how big a crib or bin. We learned how to estimate the number of shingles it would take to cover a roof, laid so many inches to the weather, or of the strips of weather-boarding for the side of a house. All the boys were interested, and most of the girls. The girls were more interested in calculations for laying carpet or putting on wallpaper. School furnished us a science for what we helped to do at home in practice. For what we might have to do when we were grown, we studied interest and promissory notes and checks and the simplest book-keeping. As a kind of adventure in arithmetic, we once organized a joint stock company and dealt in imaginary shares. Prices fluctuated by fiat of the teacher, who each day posted them on the blackboard. Guy and I bought right and left and got control. Then, again by fiat, the factory burned down, the stocks became worthless, and the undertaking ended.

I have often heard it said that in the old days people spelled more correctly than now. If this is true, it is true of older days than mine at Hope. Then, although we had a spelling match the last half-hour of many Fridays, we made the mistakes which must always be made by all but experts in the difficult English language. One winter a neighboring school held a series of public spelling bees in the evening. We thought of this as a conscious revival of a former custom. Guy and I, then perhaps eleven and thirteen, drove our bay Indian pony Dick in his red and black cart to see what the first of them would be like.

It seemed strange to be in a schoolroom at night, dark outside, dusky inside with kerosene lamps, and stranger to see men and women sitting at desks built for boys and girls. The teacher of that school took charge. About half of those who had come sat as audience. The other half chose sides and stood in lines along two walls. The teacher gave out words from a familiar spelling book, first to one side, then to the other. Each person who misspelled a word went back to his seat. When nobody was left on one side, the other was the winner. Then came the match for individuals, all in one long row. First the teacher gave us easy words. The line grew confident, and the audience restless. He turned farther toward the back of the book. Hard words thinned us out. Hard words, however, were not enough. There were wary spellers in the line. Finally he came to tricky words. The line shortened to three, a man, a woman, and a boy. He gave me the word indelible and I spelled it. Four or five turns later, he gave me deleble. I had never seen the word, spelled it by analogy with indelible, and went down. (It is a mild comfort to realize that in time delible came to be the preferred spelling.) I do not remember whether the man or the woman left was the victor.

But I remember what happened on the way home. Guy and I got away with the pony ahead of most of the others. He was trotting at his usual jog along the narrow dirt road when we heard sharp hoofs behind us. By the faint moon we could see that it was our own teacher and another man, driving the showy sorrels Dexter and Rarus to an open buggy. They swung to the left and started to pass. Dick was eighteen and lazy and fat, but he loved a race better than food or drink. Guy and I were still hot with competition. The pony broke into a run and we gave him his head. Dexter and Rarus fell back for a moment. I suspect the men were astonished, and not too sure it would be safe to race with boys so young. Then the team drew closer to us. We hogged the road without a scruple, yelled at Dick, and lashed him with the ends of the reins. He ran like a dog, head down, nose out, his belly close to the ground, his unshod feet making almost no sound. For a quarter of a mile Dexter and Rarus could not pass him, and when at last they did, they had to plunge by with two wheels dangerously in the ditch at the side of the road. Dick accepted what he could not help and, blowing noisily, lagged the rest of the way home. Guy and I were wild with a triumph we would never have felt if one of us had stood up last in the spelling match. Dick had kept ahead of Dexter and Rarus for a quarter of a mile, which was his distance. We were not so wild as to tell our parents, who would have known that racing horses in harness in the dark along a rough narrow road is one of the best ways to break a neck. And our triumph was absolute when the next day at school our teacher praised the pony.

Writing in school meant practice in penmanship and the study of the forms of correspondence. The days of copper-plate hand-writing had gone, and our grandfathers complained. In our decade we went through the general change from a slanting to a vertical hand and came out of it writing shapelessly. Grammar was formal, parsing words and analyzing sentences. Most of the children parsed and analyzed yet spoke as ungrammatically as ever, their speech rising no higher than its source at home.

As to reading, we did little in school besides the graded selections in successive readers. We read them aloud in class. We looked up the pronunciation and meaning of the hard words. The unabridged dictionary on its metal stand had definitions not only of hard but also of bad words. We hunted for all we knew, and stared at them shameless in print. What the selections we read might be about, as wholes, we hardly noticed. I remember only two. One was a passage from the Tempest which gave Guy what was long his favorite term of abuse: "Ape with forehead villainous low." Through him it entered the private vocabulary which we used only when together or, later, with our younger brothers. The second passage was from Ivanhoe, the account of the archery contest at the tournament. This was my peak of romance. I still flush with the glow of that old excitement, I still smell the book in which I read, I still see Robin Hood and his rivals exactly as I saw them then. No other narrative sentence has ever seemed to me so shining and satisfying as that final one: "His arrow split the willow rod against which it was aimed." But when I set up a peeled willow and shot at it, my arrow realistically missed.

School was less local than church. Every year there were central examinations for all the districts of the township, and final examinations for the winners from several townships. We were not required to take them, but to pass was creditable and to be first was as honorable, if not as profitable, as if Hope had been in China. I took my central examination in the ordinary routine, and was surprised when I learned I had the highest marks. The final examination became important.

It was held at Collison, which was the nearest railroad station and seven miles away. One other boy from Hope went too. That morning I got up before daylight, saddled the pony, and rode past Roy's house, where he joined me. A belated snow had fallen all night, and was still falling, so sticky that we must have looked like snow-boys on snow-horses. It balled up on our horses' feet, which we had frequently to scrape out to keep them from slipping. Roy was loose-mouthed, bragging all the way about how easily he would pass. I was nervous about myself and disgusted with him. We rode past the oak shadows of Pilot Grove and its big, quiet house. A swinging lantern moved about near the barn. I remember nothing more of the next six miles, but it was daylight when we reached Collison and stabled our horses.

Collison had a brick schoolhouse of several rooms. The contestants shuffled about the corridors until a bell called us to the day's work. Most of our teachers were there, advising and encouraging us. They got us settled at our desks, with printed questions and paper to write on. I dived into the examination and thought of nothing else for three hours.

At noon we were given an hour off and dinner, for twenty-five cents apiece, served by the ladies of the Methodist church. I liked the scalloped oysters best. We ate like school children, and went back to the examination.

During the second three hours I must have got tired, though I felt it only as impatience. A good many children had turned in their papers and left the room, to skylark in the corridors. I envied them. And I wanted, before I set out for home, to talk to Amy, a girl I liked. Though she was taking the examination, she was no scholar and had been among the first to find she had written all she knew. Seeing her at the door, teasing me, I hurried through my answers to the questions in American history, and joined her.

The teachers had read the papers as they came in, and in half an hour the marks were ready. We crowded in from the corridors. My own teacher looked sternly at me. "Don't you know what the Missouri Compromise was?" he asked. My spirit slumped. I did know, but I had overlooked the question in my hurry. A girl from another township had been more conscientious, and I came out second to her. The worst thing about it was the disappointment of my father and mother that night when I rode up in the dark and had to tell them. I did not tell them about Amy.

My family were not ready to move to town as soon as I was ready to go to high school, so that my last year at Hope would have been wasted if the new teacher had not taught me algebra and ancient history in a special class which it must have been inconvenient for him to crowd into his days. I had little sense of marking time. School was the only life I knew outside of the farm, and studies were only a part of what we did there. This was a community of children, imitating the larger community in preparation for living in it. I found it pleasant, as one of the oldest boys, to have a hand in the government, and felt authority all the more because my brothers Frank and Mark, seven and five, were among the governed. Like the other older boys, too, I discovered girls. From being nuisances they had become amusements and mysteries. We talked about them a great deal, speculating. One of the girls in the neighborhood that spring climbed out a window at night and eloped with the hired man. Her father went after her and brought her back. The children hardly mentioned it to their parents, but the scandal cannot have hummed more busily anywhere than it did at school.

The boys and girls who had done the work of the eight grades were ready for whatever the community demanded, except experience. Most of the girls married early. The ambitious boys went further with their schooling, prepared to go as far as they chose. Of the five sons of a family in the next district and the five in my family, nine went to college; two became college professors, two agricultural experts, two writers, one an architect, one a broker, one a merchant, and one a salesman. Of the rest, the majority became farmers. I have never heard that any one of them all ever complained that his first school had done less for him than it should.

4

HOPE was so self-contained, and I was so young when we lived there, that I observed almost nothing of its relations to the county and the state. My father was a member of the school board, but this to me meant only that we got free passes—once to a demonstration of the incredible phonograph which some traveling entertainer gave in the schoolhouse, and once to a medicine show which pitched its tent on the school grounds for a week. A great-uncle of mine, a township supervisor, had something to do with the county poor. I remember when I first learned the meaning of the word pauper, and wondered if I would ever see such a person. I used to hear some comment now and then on the political ring which administered the county at Danville. When our teacher left Hope to become county superintendent of schools, we admired him. The state was too large to interest me more than vaguely, though I went with my father and mother and Guy to the World's Fair in Chicago, to be worn out with dazzling wonders, and though I listened to violent abuse of Governor Altgeld when he pardoned the Chicago anarchists.

Our community was almost entirely Republican. Its political hero was Speaker Cannon of the House of Representatives. Vermilion County called him Uncle Joe, and when he came, as he often did, to speak at Potomac, twelve miles away, he was very friendly with my grandfather, whom Potomac called Uncle Jerry. They had known each other from boyhood in the pioneer time. They even looked alike, as I used to think so many men of their generation did, although the Speaker was a politician, and my grandfather fastidious and fanatical.

During the Presidential campaign of 1892 some of the boys wore stiff, ugly caps which had Cleveland or Harrison printed across the front, and little Republicans taunted little Democrats in doggerel:

"How big is Grover Cleveland, Pa, that people call him great?
Is he as big as Uncle Ben, the favorite candidate?"
"Oh, no, my son, he weighs a ton, but mostly gall and fat.
He wears a number nineteen collar and a little Tom Thumb hat."

After Cleveland was elected the Republicans in Hope proph-
esied the worst, and they blamed him for all that happened in
1893.

I was not affected. I ate, dressed, slept, played, and read
exactly as I would have done if there had been no crisis. That
winter, or the next, we once or twice burned corn in the
Round Oak stove and talked about the hot, oily fire it made.
A new standing joke appeared in the community. Some man,
it was said, had sent a carload of sheep to Chicago. The com-
mission agent reported that the amount received for them
would not pay the railroad charges, and asked for money to
make up the loss. The man replied: "Have no money, but
am sending more sheep." No matter how often we heard
this, we laughed. The general distress pinched our community but did not overwhelm it. What was going on in in-
dustrial cities, we did not guess. The horror that came nearest
to us was in Kansas, which grew to a legend.

Although I have since then often been in Kansas, I can
never lose my childish picture of it as a treeless plain, bare
from drought, swept with hot winds, eaten up by chinch bugs.
Bleeding Kansas. Starving Kansas. Burning Kansas. Several
families had gone from Hope to that cheaper land, and letters as well as newspapers told us about it. Now and then
movers, as we called them, in covered wagons, went misera-
bly past our house. I remember a wagon which had, daubed
on the canvas, the defeated but rebellious words:

I'm tired of Kansas and starvation.
I'm going back to my wife's relations.
Damn Cleveland's administration.

Many of the movers stopped to beg, clumsily, for food and
fodder. We always gave it to them, and heard their stories.
One pitiful woman, the first dirty woman Guy and I had
ever seen, whined when my mother asked her if she could
use a side of salt pork and a sack of corn meal: "I'd be glad
to get anything." Her answer must have struck Guy, for that
night at supper, when asked what he would have, he said
the same words in nearly the same tone. "I'd be glad to get
anything," whined, became a household sentence. We were
not a heartless family, but we had had no experience of
want to the point of actual hunger, and the sight of it could
not sadden us long.

The Spanish-American war was an explosion and a blaze
on the horizon. Nobody that I knew went from Hope to be
a soldier, and nobody argued intelligently about the war's
origin or purpose. It came to us as simple melodrama in the
newspapers. In the lovely island of Cuba, which many of us
for the first time learned was in the West Indies and belonged
to Spain, an innocent people were brutally oppressed by
tyrants from the Old Country—our common name for Eu-
rope. How vile these tyrants were had not been realized until
they blew up the Maine. Now that the truth was known,
our duty to free the Cubans from their yoke was as strong as
the need to punish them for their murderous treachery to us.
This was like the Revolution, which had freed the American
colonists from Great Britain. This was like the Civil War,
which had freed the slaves. The pulse of altruism throbbed
in our veins. Once more the righteous had taken arms against
the wicked. Not for years afterward did I, or I suppose any

other native of the village, regard the war with critical eyes. We believed what the newspapers told us to believe, and read nothing between their uninformed, or interested, or sinister lines. A selfish war was supported by a generous people.

In that feverish spring the past rose to a fresh life among us. Only the old remembered war. For the young, war existed in books. When it appeared in newspapers it seemed to bring something of the past with it. War was history. This was war. Therefore, this was history. The instinctive syllogism had a magic influence. It enlarged the conflict into something heroic. I did not see a single uniform or flag or rifle in Hope, but when I read the papers I was looking, I dimly felt, at history as a reality. My world, becoming wider, became deeper, touched with a large illusion. The scuffles in Cuba, the crashing assault on Manila, the breathless voyage of the Oregon around the Cape, the massacre of the Spanish fleet: these gave us epic days. Nor was this at all peculiar to me or the children of my age. The run of historical fiction which followed took countless American readers back over the whole American past. Almost as if the shabby war wished to hide its dubious face, it threw out bright, soft, sweet clouds of romance.

The facts of the war interested us, not the debates of the treaty and the peace. Those who opposed expansion into the West Indies and the Philippines were held to be a pedantic, if not an unpatriotic, crew absurdly bent on turning the clock of time back. The United States had already expanded. It was too late to wrangle. The nation's destiny was manifest, white man's burden and all. Democracy had triumphed in America for a century, and now had triumphed over a European foe. The future was immense and secure.

5

IN 1933 I motored through Hope on a broad, swift highway running straight north to Chicago. My brother Paul, born at Hope, but only a year old when we moved away, drove so fast that we were upon the village before I expected to be and beyond it before I could take in more than flickering images of the church and the house where I was born. As we rushed on under the maples my grandfather had set out on both sides of the road along his farm, I looked back half-bewildered. Most of the houses were gone. Not a soul that I had known still lived there. The very name of the village had been lost since the post office was given up. Hope is a gray monument. A stranger might go by without ever suspecting that it was once the center of life for its own society. Yet there a microcosm formed and dissolved, and there the essential story of an older America was compressed into three generations.

Two of my great-grandfathers had come to Pilot township before the Civil War. The Butzes were of Pennsylvania German stock from another Hope, in New Jersey, where my grandfather was born. While he was still a child, his father read a book about the West that stirred him, and he fell in with the movement that shifted a whole people during the Jacksonian days. The family went first to Ohio, near Sandusky, and then on to Illinois, near Decatur. From there, for some reason, my Great-grandfather Butz turned back to Vermilion County, to settle at Hope. My grandfather, driving a yoke of oxen to a wagon loaded with farm tools, almost lost them crossing an unbridged stream at the spot where

Urbana later built the high school in which I, still later, peacefully studied. A boy shouting at his oxen mired down in the ford. A boy reading about the wars in Gaul. The same place, and only fifty years between.

Pilot township already had a few inhabitants who seem to have been lost in the prairie sloughs. They had not, like some of their friends, settled in the timber along the Middle Fork, holding that only land which would grow trees would grow crops. But, settled around Hope, they had found that the soil, however fertile, needed to be drained if they were not to live half the year in mud. When my great-grandfather came, they lived in mud, desolately. The first thing they asked of him was that he should make forceps and pull their teeth, which had had to ache till they stopped aching or fell out. He was a blacksmith, not a dentist, but he made the forceps and pulled the teeth.

With drainage, the prairie people soon left the timber people behind. To live down in the timber in my day was to be thought wild and backward. They used to tell the story of a man who had lived there, long before, and who never came out except on election day. Then, year after year, he would emerge, coonskin on his head, rifle across his shoulder, and make his way to the polls. Coming up to the judges of the election he invariably said:

"I cast one vote for Andy Jackson."

"But Andy Jackson," he would be told, "is not a candidate."

"Makes no difference. I cast one vote for Andy Jackson."

After Jackson's death the man from the timber would not change his vote.

"I cast one vote for Andy Jackson."

"Andy Jackson is dead. You can't vote for him."

"It's a damned Whig lie. Andy Jackson will live forever. I cast one vote for Andy Jackson."

The Tillotsons were prairie people. In the seventeenth century a Tillotson had been Archbishop of Canterbury and had written, John Dryden thought, the first modern English prose. Another Tillotson preferred Massachusetts to England. From New England certain Tillotsons spilled over into New York, where one of them married a woman, my great-great-grandmother, who brought into the family some of the blood of one of the Six Nations. My Great-grandfather Tillotson looked almost as much Indian as Puritan, austere and proud. My grandmother, born in Indiana, had from this Red strain her high cheek-bones and perhaps her stoic silence. The Tillotsons, who settled north of Hope, became the largest and the most permanent clan in the township. The country between Hope and Armstrong swarmed with my great-aunts and great-uncles and their many children, and the annual reunion of the Tillotsons and their kin to this day brings scores and even hundreds together, few of whom come from more than fifty miles away.

When Jeremiah Butz went to the father of Rebecca Tillotson to ask for her in marriage, he found the older man chopping wood. The young man was timid, not only because he was at a natural disadvantage, but also because he could not help knowing that the substantial Tillotsons might well consider the Butzes a restless lot. He had to force himself to say what he had come for.

"Mr. Tillotson, we—that is, Becky and I—we—we think it may be foolish, but we think—we think we would like to get married."

The old gentleman went on with his ax, as if waiting for

more. My grandfather was too much frightened to speak.
Finally, between strokes, the father said:

"If you think it is foolish, why do you want to do it?"
And he said nothing else.

There seemed to the lovers nothing to do but run away.
They drove to Danville, to a fair, got their license, happened
to see a justice of the peace they knew, asked him to marry
them, and, sitting in a buggy, were married by the justice,
standing beside it. My grandfather, having persuaded my
grandmother this far, coaxed her into what followed. They
hurried home before the others, and when the substantial
Tillotsons came in, wondering about Rebecca, they found
her already in bed with a man who they did not yet know
was her husband.

My grandfather's brothers were restless enough. Two of
them moved on to Kansas, then to Idaho, and one of them
to British Columbia. When he was an old man he wrote a
letter in which he said he had gone as far as he could on
the American continent, and had decided he would go no
farther west till he went to heaven. But my grandfather was
more stable, and he was married to a Tillotson. He lived for
almost forty years on one farm, retired to Potomac, and
lived for over thirty years more in the same house. His four
sons, three of whom looked like Tillotsons, as soon as they
were men all made for the Indian Territory, where the two
younger married women who were both part Cherokee.

My grandfather and grandmother established themselves
on the farm that lay nearest to Hope on the north and east.
From him I picked up all I know about the life of his generation.

He broke the prairie sod, driving five yoke of straining

oxen, stopping every hour or so to hammer the iron plow-
share to a sharper edge. Some of the grass roots, immemorial,
were as thick as his arm. He said it was like plowing through
a heavy woven door-mat. He dug hundreds of rods of drainage ditch, making the tile himself. He fenced part of his land
with rails brought from the timber. It was a day's work to
go, split the rails for a rod of fence, and bring them back.
He was one of the first to realize that the thorny osage
orange would make good hedges, and to begin setting out
the plants and waiting for them to grow. Remembering New
Jersey, he collected and hoarded stone for years, until he
had enough to lay a foundation for his barn. In those old
times, he said, the deer were so plentiful that a man could
stand on rising ground and at a distance see droves of them.
One day in winter, when the prairie was covered with a
sheet of ice, two or three men went out with a hayrack on
a sled and brought back a load of deer which they had killed
without firing a shot. The dogs chased them, the deer slipped
and fell on the ice, and the men cut their throats.

My grandfather lived with his growing family for some
years in a prairie cabin which, after he built a permanent
house, was given over to the chickens. He used to tease me
by saying that my mother, his third child, had been born in
a hen-coop. The work he and my grandmother did must
have been terrific, and harder on her than on him. She bore
the children and took the burden of his impetuous hospi-
tality. Once, when he brought a raft of visitors home for
dinner, unexpected, she had nothing to give them but green
corn, of which she and the girls cooked enough to fill a wash
tub. But he did not spare himself. Besides all the work he
had to do, he invented other work. There was the long ave-

nue of maples he set out. It was his boast that after he was twenty-one he never let a year go by without planting trees. And he was, as the county history called him, the elegant man of Pilot township, forever busy with improving his farm and trying to improve the community. In his later years he made his house and grounds in Potomac a gardener's paradise. He argued for hard roads, for an electric railway. He wasted money boring for oil. The older he grew the bolder he was. When he was a young man he would have knocked down anybody who had called him an Abolitionist. When he was an old man, he was a Prohibitionist. Thousands of times he declared he would never cast his vote for any party that would license an evil for revenue. When he ran for Coroner on the county ticket, he announced that if elected he would bury Republicans and Democrats with equal pleasure.

He was like most men of his generation in that older America. He looked upon the future as a perpetual adventure and never doubted that it was an endless source of benefits to come. Men had only to work and wait for them. He had seen the wild prairie blossom under his hands. Other men could do and see as much if they chose. His contemporaries at Hope, though no one of them was quite so given up to the future as my grandfather, held his general opinions. They were solid, civil squires who had prospered, whose land by 1890 was worth forty times what it had been when they had claimed it from the Government, and who had never heard of any law of diminishing returns. At the same time, they doubted that the generation of their sons, who were to inherit these farms already plowed and drained and hedged, could ever match the fathers. The old men had a

kind of patriarchal status. Every year at the Old Settlers'
Day celebration they listened with pride to stories of times
past, much as more ancient patriarchs must have listened to
stories of the conquest of Canaan.

My father, who belonged to the generation of the sons,
was in a sense as much a pioneer as any of the fathers. He
was not a native of Hope, but settled there, as the one
physician for miles around, after the community had been
formed. He came from Kankakee County, where his father
was both preacher and farmer. My Great-grandfather Van
Doren had been the first of his Dutch line to leave New
Jersey, first for New York State, where my grandfather was
born, and then for Illinois. My father, while like all the Van
Dorens before him he felt he must own land, like most of
them also studied a profession, to earn more money to buy
land. At the medical school in Chicago he might have been
a Scottish student in Edinburgh, not only supported by the
farm at home but actually fed in part on food sent from it.
He began the practice of medicine as assistant to his elder
brother Silas at Penfield, a dozen miles away from Hope,
and came there on the urging of various men, including my
Grandfather Butz, who felt that Hope ought to have a doctor of its own. My father's fortune was then his clothes, his
medicine kit, and a black saddle-horse.

When, that winter, the community Christmas tree was
being set up in the church and hung with presents, he
dropped in with those he was to give, and slyly tucked in
somewhere a silk handkerchief for himself. Hardly more
than a boy, he could not bear to seem neglected when the
presents were given out, and so be marked as an outsider.
He made his way to a place in the life of Hope which only
a country doctor could have had. If there were doubts of

him because he was young, they soon passed. One of his earliest patients was my Uncle Mark, a giant at seventeen, who had an attack of spinal meningitis in the night and was found in convulsions in a bed he had broken to pieces. When he got well the credit went to my father. Two years after he came to Hope he was married to my mother.

She was as ambitious as he. At ten she had ridden back and forth across the prairie with the mail-bags for the village, when my grandfather was postmaster. At fifteen she had begun to teach school. Though she had had only one year at a normal college, she was at twenty the best-educated girl in Hope, as my father was the best-educated man. But they were both too much at home there to think for years of leaving. They built a house in the village, where two sons were born. My father's growing practice and my mother's growing household were not enough. They bought a farm west of Hope and moved to it. For ten years, during which three more sons were born, they matched the pioneers for labor.

They lived in a comfortable house instead of a shack. They drove a carriage instead of a wagon. They had, from my father's practice, an income outside of the farm. It took them only that ten years, as against my grandfather's and grandmother's forty, to find themselves able to retire. Yet what they did was terrific too. Indoors my mother never had more than one servant—hired girl—if she had one, and outdoors my father had to run the farm in the intervals of a practice which never allowed him an hour in which he might not be called away. The scale of his farming was larger than Hope had been used to, the pace faster. He put in as many tile as the farm's former owner. He did more to better the fertility of the soil. He built more barns and sheds.

He raised more livestock. He paid more attention to markets and Government reports, of which there were now more to pay attention to. In the end, his ambition outran my mother's, or at least became different. She valued his profession most, and wanted him to advance in it. He was absorbed in the land and believed in its future with a stubborn optimism.

But times were changing and my brothers and I were growing old enough for other schools. The boys of the neighborhood, as much used to horses as to their own legs, rushed about on bicycles, hating the hedges and the thorns which punctured tires. Two of the young women had even been seen in bloomers. An automobile—still called a horseless carriage—had driven up to ask help from the blacksmith. The telephone was coming to Hope. At our house, at least, there was an obscure sense that an age had ended. My great-grandfather had been a pioneer, my grandfather a squire. My father was ready to be a landlord and a capitalist. Rising prices and machinery had freed us to take our place with other such freedmen in the towns.

On a day in August 1900 we were startled by a long line of carriages and buggies coming toward the farm from the village. It was a surprise party, Hope's farewell to my mother and father. Almost everybody we knew piled out, and teams were hitched to the fence the whole length of the lane. Before we quite knew what had happened, the men had set up trestles and a long table on the lawn, and the women had unpacked baskets of such food as belonged to Fourth of July celebrations and Old Settlers' Day: roast chicken, fried chicken, boiled chicken with dumplings, pressed chicken in jelly, young turkey, guinea hen (red meat was for cold seasons); smearcase, hardboiled eggs, deviled eggs, pickled

eggs; potato salad, bowls of lettuce with cream and vinegar
dressing, pickled beets, pickled onions, green peppers stuffed
with piccalilli, sour cucumbers, sweet cucumbers, mixed
pickles; light bread, light biscuits, soda biscuits, salt rising
bread, corn bread, raisin bread, nut bread; sun-preserved
cherries, preserved strawberries and raspberries and blackberries and plums, pickled peaches, apple sauce, apple butter, peach butter, grape butter, stewed pears, apple jelly, currant jelly, apple and currant jelly, grape jelly, watermelon
preserves, tomato preserves; layer cakes with white or cara-
mel or chocolate icing, cakes with chopped walnuts or hick-
ory nuts or butternuts in the layers or between them, marble
cakes, cakes with lemon icing or red sugar on top, fruit cakes
rich with citron, angel food, devil's food, cup cakes, dough-
nuts, crullers, cookies; fresh apple pie, dried apple pie, cherry
pie, blackberry pie, gooseberry pie, gooseberry and currant
pie, raisin pie, lemon pie, rhubarb pie. One man brought a
wagon-load of watermelons. And, since these were modern
times and Hope now had an ice-house, there were freezers
of ice cream and gallons of lemonade.

We ate. Then speeches, laughter, tears, and endless talking all over the house and grounds until the guests had to
go home. It was long before I realized what the occasion
must have meant to my family and the community. At the
time, my flushed pride was mixed with disgust for the tears.
Seeing that my father and mother were moved, I told myself
they were old—he was forty-three, she thirty-seven—and soft.
Our ten years on the farm, I thought, were something to be
left behind with the farm, decisively.

6

WHEN we moved from the village to the farm I was five, and I remember sitting on top of a load of furniture and poking at the clock so that it struck all the way there. At the next step of my memory we seem to have been as thoroughly rooted in the farm as its trees.

Between the white house and the road there was a kind of park, surrounded by a high paneled fence and planted with hard and soft maples, elms, and cedars. Among them were mulberry, pear, and plum trees, and a thicket of wild plums, and along one side, just outside the fence, a row of cherry trees from which we used to scare robins and blue jays when the fruit was ripe. The house stood in a smaller yard with a picket fence which protected its lilacs, mock oranges, peonies, asparagus, and beds of flowers from the sheep which were now and then turned into the park to keep the grass down. To the left of the house, as you faced it from the road, lay first the vegetable garden and then the orchard, and behind the house the truck garden. Beyond the orchard and the truck garden, to the west and north of the house, which fronted south to the road but had its chief entrance on the east, were artificial groves of willow, ash, and walnut, with long rows of osage orange which had been allowed to grow for fence posts. The former owner had turned a part of the prairie into a wood. My brothers and I spent almost as many hours of our summer days in the trees as under them. I still remember the shock I felt when my father allowed one of the cedars to be cut down for the church's Christmas tree.

We seldom used the driveway through the park, prefer-
ring the farm lane which, with no gate to open at the road,
led past the house to the stables at the rear. To the right of
the lane was the little pasture, for the pony and the horses
my father used to ride or drive to see his patients, and behind that the big pasture, for the cows, the work horses and
mules, and whatever other stock might need it. All the rest
of the farm was field or meadow, every square rod culti-
vated except the small plot where the foreman lived. He
was not quite a foreman, but a married man hired by the
year to carry out my father's orders with the help of the
unmarried men who came and went in varying numbers
with the seasons.

For the whole decade of the nineties we lived there almost
as independent of the world at large as if this had been still
the eighteenth century. The general store in the village had
staple groceries and sometimes oranges, lemons, and bananas.
From the nearest butchers, miles away, my father, if he had
been to Ogden, Fithian, Collison, Potomac, or Armstrong
on business, might bring home fresh meat as a summer lux-
ury. But whatever else we ate came from the farm.

We had beef when the winter cold would keep a slaugh-
tered steer till we, and probably some other family who
shared the cost, could eat the whole of it. Mutton, on our
farm, was more common. When I was fourteen I could kill,
skin, clean, and hang a wether in thirty minutes. Pork and
chicken we had oftenest of all. No day of the year ever
stirred my brothers and me more than the day we butchered.
The men built a fire under a caldron standing on iron legs
in the barnyard, and set up a wooden platform beside it. The
hogs, dragged from the pen, squealed wildly while they were
stuck and bled. Bloody hands plunged the fat dead bodies

in the boiling water, lifted them on the platform, and scraped the bristles off with the edge of a corn-knife. Butcher knives, sharpened while the water boiled, cut up the carcasses. Part of the meat was saved to be eaten fresh or ground up into sausage. Hams went to the smoke house, sides to casks of brine, bellies and the waste to kettles to be rendered into lard or boiled down to soap fat. It took the whole household days to dispose of what the men got ready for us in half a day. Killing chickens was a lighter matter. A stealthy visit to the roost at night or a short chase by day, squawks, an expert wringing of a neck, a headless flopping on the ground, hot water and wet feathers, a knife to open the bird and find the joints: a few minutes were enough, and few days went by without such minutes. When we said "squeal like a stuck hog" or "run around like a chicken with its head off" we were taking our similes from life.

Bakers were as far away as butchers. Our own oven furnished all our bread, which we liked best to eat when it was so hot that butter would melt into it as into a sponge. So with all the kinds of biscuit and corn bread. The oven was never idle. Cakes and pies poured out of it. The pantry—always called the buttery—had a special box for cakes, a rack for pies, and a stone jar for cookies. My brothers and I were not supposed to cut a cake or pie without permission, but we had the run of the cooky jar.

So long as we lived at Hope I never even heard of buying vegetables or salad at a market. Our green season began with the first rhubarb, of which we knew that name although we usually called it pie plant. After a winter diet, rhubarb was such a delight it seemed a tonic. Then, in turn, radishes, lettuce, young onions, peas, string beans, wax beans, tomatoes, celery, parsnips, cabbage, turnips, from the vegetable garden, and from the truck garden strawberries, raspberries, blackberries, new potatoes, and roasting ears. From the earliest cherries to the latest winter apples some fruit or other was always ripe. And at the end of the season there were pumpkins between the corn rows.

"We eat what we can, and what we can't eat we can," said a country jingle. Knowing we could buy nothing fresh out of season, we had to save for winter what the summer had left behind. In the fall we plowed up bushels of potatoes and picked barrels of apples for the cellar, where kegs of sauerkraut stood beside casks of salt pork. Other apples were buried in beds of straw in pits dug in the vegetable garden. We put up few vegetables but hundreds of glass jars of fruit and preserves, which filled shelf after shelf on the cellar wall. We dried apples and the cooked meat of pumpkins. Then we settled to our winter fare: meat and potatoes, bread and gravy, canned corn and canned tomatoes, pickles and preserves, pies and cakes. We were always greedy for anything made from corn grown and ground on the farm: mush and milk, fried mush, corn bread, corn-meal cakes, and lye hominy. Our hominy, in ten-gallon jars, was left in the summer kitchen to freeze and thaw till it was tender. Weeks of this winter fare, and then rhubarb again. If the food was monotonous, we did not know it.

With some help from visiting dress-makers my mother made most of her own clothes and clothes for the boys when they were babies. When we were older, some of our shirts were made at home, and sometimes our heavy woolen stockings. From the village store we got rough straw hats for summer, fleece-lined caps and mittens for winter, rubber boots for spring and fall, and overalls for every day. The rest of our clothing came from Danville or—ordered by mail—

from Chicago. We even had smart tweed suits from the Lili-
putian Bazaar in New York. I admired them, but was em-
barrassed when the other boys thought they were stuck-up.
We suffered now and then from my mother's taste. She
would not let us wear high boots with brass-bound toes, or
felt boots with rubber overshoes, or exposed suspenders. She
made us put on overcoats on days when we felt it would be
manlier to do without. Once she insisted that I go to school
in a new pair of buttoned shoes which I was sure looked like
a girl's. I sat at my desk all through the noon hour, refusing
to join the other children in the playground for fear they
might ridicule my shoes. But I seldom thought more about
my clothing than if I had been a colt. Like a colt, I was un-
comfortable, at least in warm weather, when I was forced
to wear shoes. Everything else I took for granted, outgrew
it, and passed it on to my younger brothers.

We were a masculine household, and I do not remember
a single dress my mother wore while we lived at Hope,
though I do remember words I heard her and her friends
use: basque, bodice, sacque, front breadth, panel, hemstitch,
featherstitch, basting, pleat, gore, ruching, tuck, bombazine,
calico, gingham, silk, satin, tulle, voile, cambric, challis, rib-
bon, lace, fast color, leg-of-mutton sleeve, sash, shawl, corset,
V-front, crochet, appliqué, Mother Hubbard (of which my
mother disapproved), shirt waist, insertion, bustle, petticoat,
chemise, drawers, mitts, broadcloth. The tumbled words are
clearer in my memory than the things they stood for. The
one garment of my mother's which I remember is a long
gray shawl she wore one day when she drove Guy and me
to my grandfather's in Potomac. It was a cool day, and the
broncos, Dandy and Nelly, were skittish. Arrived at the
hitch-rack in front of the house, my mother got out and

went to tie the off horse first. Dandy was wild, and the wind blew her shawl in his eyes. He wheeled, taking the gentler Nelly with him, and ran off down the road, with the two little boys screaming in the seat. The horses turned in at the barn, and one of the men caught them. I can still see the shawl whip upward in the wind. After that my mother was never quite so bold a horsewoman as she had been all her life.

The fashions in women's clothing must have changed, but I did not notice that, any more than I noticed that the fashions in boys' clothing changed hardly at all, except as boys grew older and, at about twelve, rose from knee breeches to long trousers. My father, less concerned than any of us about his clothes, seems to me now to have changed most during our ten years on the farm. His high hat gave way to a derby and then to a fedora; his Prince Albert coat to a cutaway and then to a sack; his stiff-bosomed shirts to soft shirts, though with stiff cuffs and collars. He always wore a doctor's clothes, not a farmer's, and when he took a hand on the farm, he did it in old clothes. Work clothes in Hope were likely to be old clothes. A man might scatter manure in a frock-coat, green with age, which had once been black and his Sunday best.

Indoors, my father had an office in the lower floor of one wing of the house, cut off from the rest by a hall and stairway. There he saw his patients, and there, behind a partition in one corner, he put up their medicines. He pulled aching teeth, set dislocated joints, bound fractured bones in primitive splints. Sometimes he had an assistant, always a young doctor just out of medical school who had not yet found a practice of his own. Sometimes I was my father's assistant, whittling splints out of smooth pine or holding bandages.

Once, when he removed dangerous tonsils from a boy of about my age, I dropped the chloroform on the mask which my father held, and later pinned the boy's hands down during the operation. In an emergency, my father might be called on for anything. He was Hope's only specialist, as well as its only practitioner. He was also its only veterinary, though most of the farmers knew how to treat their own sick animals. Guy, resentful because my father was away so much of the time seeing sick people, once wished he were a cow doctor.

A French observer of life in the United States declares that he found in the families of country doctors the sole American instance of something like an hereditary profession, almost an hereditary rank. While two of my father's brothers were country doctors and one had been at a medical school when he died, and another was a pharmacist, none of my brothers studied medicine. But our whole family had, I think, an obscure sense of being set a little apart by the profession. I felt half-guilty when I decided I did not want to be a doctor. The same thing happened to another boy, also the son of a country doctor, at about the same time in Minnesota. I think it is fair to guess that behind the passion which drove Martin Arrowsmith in his career lay a dim sense of guilt in Sinclair Lewis. Because he was not a doctor himself, he had to imagine his doctor-hero to the uttermost, as a kind of apology and tribute to the profession he felt he had deserted.

My father must have been at home a good deal, but I remember him as forever going and coming, particularly going out in black nights which, when I was small, frightened me. Now and then, when he was treating some infectious disease, he would not let us come near him, but as a rule we swarmed around and over him like puppies, for he was amiable, gay, and patient. He seemed never to be tired. After being away all night, he would drop down on a couch, even with the boys playing in the room on a rainy day, sleep for a quarter of an hour, and wake up a new man. He seldom forgot to bring us candy from the village. When we were expecting him, we used to wait at the mouth of the lane, our eyes on the point of the road from which he could first see us. If he had forgotten, he would, however wearily, turn his powerful, hard-gaited gray horse—Prince or Billy—around and gallop back to the store. Then we would run shouting to meet him.

The formal parlor had the marble-topped center-table that most parlors had, a cottage organ, and bookshelves covering half of one wall. Guy and I took our music lessons there, resisting music, which we thought girlish, until my mother gave up hope in us. We often read in the parlor, sprawled on the ingrain carpet which was comfortably padded underneath with a layer of straw. Heated by an open fireplace, where a fire was rarely built, the parlor was likely to be cold except in summer. It was a ceremonial room. But I there came as close to violent death as I ever came. When I was still small enough to wear a pinafore, I tried to reach something from the mantel, set fire to my clothing, and ran in flames and terror to my mother, who threw me down and rolled me in a rug.

My father's office had a small stove and the kitchen of course a cookstove. The rest of the house depended on the sitting-room, with its omnivorous Round Oak which overheated that room and had something to spare, through open doors, for the parlor and dining-room, and, through iron registers in the ceiling, for the bedrooms upstairs. We went upstairs only to sleep. In cold weather, my brothers and I undressed beside the stove, and then ran up the shivering stairway to our icy beds, which in the coldest weather had had the chill taken off by hot bricks wrapped in rags. Our baths we took in a wash tub in the warm kitchen after supper.

Of the house's dozen rooms, we chiefly lived in three, and the three were really one, for the dining-room was hardly more than a broad passage between the sitting-room and the kitchen. I remember the kitchen best of all, with its smell of food, and the cheerful simmering of the kettle. Our kitchen was unlike anybody else's, for the windmill stood so close to the kitchen wall that we could open a casement window to get a fresh drink from the hogshead into which the mill pumped cool hard water. From the hogshead the waste water overflowed through a pipe to the milk-trough in the buttery, with its crocks of milk and cream, and murmured out through the drain. I know now that the mill ran only when there was wind and we needed water, but I seem, remembering, to hear always the creak and hum of the wheel and the clank of the shaft—though I remember, too, the still days when we had to disconnect the windmill and pump water by hand, not only for the house but also for the horse-tank in the barnyard.

From the small brick-paved court behind the kitchen Guy and I used to climb the windmill ladder, crawl around the frame to the kitchen roof, and scramble up the shingles to our bedroom window. Nothing about the house is so vivid to me, after these years, as that little court, where on summer evenings we sat on the edge of the porch and washed our feet in a tin basin, slopping the water carelessly on the worn red bricks. To this day, when I have to determine the points of the compass anywhere, I imagine myself back on the porch, always sitting with bare feet, looking up the long moraine toward what is for me the eternal North, with the village of Hope on my right, toward the eternal East.

7

TEN years, remembered, pour over me like a tide. Separate then, they have been mixed by time into one general memory. My life on the farm seems to be not so much an experience ten years long as a spacious moment in which everything happened at once. I can remember when Frank and Mark and Paul were born, but I find it hard to remember when they had not yet been. Unless I force my reason to correct my sight, I see us as always seven. My father and mother, called Papa and Mamma. Guy and I, called the big boys. Frank and Mark, the little boys. Paul, the baby. We lived together in a busy tumult, in a close-knit affection which the later scattering of the family has never weakened.

When I tell most of my friends that I had a happy childhood, I perceive that many of them are envious, more of them skeptical. It has become as common to abuse families as it used to be to exalt and sentimentalize them. An unhappy childhood is rated as an asset, like a lost love: something to be hugged. Without saying how he suffered as a child, who can hint how sensitive he is? Who can prove he is original now without recalling that he was rebellious then? On that lewd scapegoat, the family, its members heap their sins. I know there are unhappy families, tyrannical fathers, nagging mothers, quarrelsome brothers and sisters. There were unhappy families at Hope, cats and dogs, bears and monkeys. But I no more believe that families in general are as unhappy as most of my friends make out than I believe that families in general are as happy as Dickens and Thackeray insisted. In any case, I am not generalizing. I had a happy childhood in a happy family. My father was no tyrant. My mother, while sharp and quick in punishment, did not nag. And though my brothers and I often fought together, we fought, not sulked, and never carried a grudge over to the next fight. If I had to go today to a lone island with one companion, there is no living man I should prefer to any of my four brothers—though I should not know how to choose which one of them.

The years at Hope, remembered more intently, seem less like a single tide than like a slow, steady wheel, turning through the seasons.

I remember early days in June. Along with the whole family, I got up at dawn. My father, if he had not been away all night, as he often was, rode over the farm or made plans with the men. My mother set about breakfast. The little boys rushed out of the house to play. Guy did various chores, and I went to drive up the cows, my special chore. In those fresh dawns nothing was pleasanter than to find a cow still lying down and, after I had roused her, to step from the cold grass into the warm spot where she had lain. I followed the cows at their sluggish, wandering gait to the cowshed, where they went to their own stanchions and waited ruminantly for me to milk them.

To have to milk two or three cows morning and evening is to be a slave to them, I know, but I felt my slavery less than my pride in being the eldest brother and bearing this responsibility. And I enjoyed milking, even the cantankerous, tough-uddered old Shorthorn and the Jersey that kicked like a horse. Milking would give me, I had been told, a strong grip. Milking was a good time for oratory. Squatting on a three-legged stool, my head pressed against the cow's flank but my eyes alert for her lashing tail, I made up patriotic speeches, orotund and magniloquent. "By the might of his own intellect," one sentence began with a rising inflection, "and by the power of his own will," it went on with a dying fall, "Abraham Lincoln rose to the highest level in the land," with a ringing statement. I remember no more of it.

Meanwhile the men were feeding, currying, and harnessing the work horses in the barn. I could hear the horses biting at their ears of corn and stamping at the flies, the men pounding their curry combs and loudly ordering the horses to stand over.

With full pails, I went in to breakfast, after washing my hands in a basin outside the kitchen door. Breakfast was much the same as any other meal, except that it included no dessert. We ate less for refreshment after sleep than for strength for the day ahead. I hurried to the barn, led out my team, snapped their reins together, and drove them to the cornfield where I had left my plow standing the night before.

It was now six o'clock. For five hours I steered the plow back and forth along the rows, turning the grass and weeds up to the deadly sun, and leaving a wake of warm, mellow loam for my bare feet. From eleven to one I stopped work for food and a longer rest than most farmers took. Then back to the field till six again. The first hours of the afternoon were the most trying of the day, the horses lagging under the relentless sky, waves of heat rising visibly from the ground. I went again and again to the jug of water left in the shade of the hedge. Later, when the sun began to turn red, a breeze stirred the still air. Horses and boy got a kind of second wind, plowed their final rows at a quicker pace, and came back to supper at a trot.

After I had unharnessed and fed my team, milked the cows which the little boys had brought in from the pasture, eaten my supper, turned out the cows and horses, I must have been tired as I sprawled on the grass under a tree beside the house, but I remember only a gorged, happy languor in which my mood expanded with the shadows. Not even the close, hot nights of Illinois kept me from sleep when I went to bed at eight.

On the Fourth of July we got up as early as on a work day and drove in the carriage to Potomac for the celebration. Most people went directly to the picnic grounds, in a grove just west of town. We went first to my grandfather's, left the team in his stable, out of reach of firecrackers, and walked the rest of the way. The official part of the celebration was always the same. On a raised platform, draped with bunting and a flag, the same kind of orator made the same kind of speech. On hard plank benches the same audience listened with the same nods of agreement. The same band played badly the same anthem which the same patriots sang worse. The place of the ceremony was a sober oasis in a desert of hilarious noise: the crack and rattle of small crackers, the roar of giant crackers, the bang of torpedoes, the whine of balloon whistles, the call of hawkers and barkers at the stands, the stamping and whinnying of horses tied at the racks, babies crying, boys shouting. The smells of the day were as insistent as its sounds: bruised grass and broken weeds underfoot, popcorn and peanuts, acrid dust, horse dung, and patriotic gunpowder everywhere.

After the speaking, the plank benches were shoved together to make tables, stuffed baskets came from the carriages, and enormous meals appeared. Families ate in clans, we with the multitudinous Tillotsons. Later came a baseball game, some sly courting, much talking, and at last the tired hour, hated by boys and girls, at which the annual ecstasy started to break up. Most of the country people went home for milking. We stayed at my grandfather's house for supper, watched the fireworks, and drove back to Hope under the stars which we seldom saw in summer. I remember the night when I kept awake the whole trip and discovered that Potomac's moon was Hope's moon too.

By the Fourth the corn was generally laid by, and we turned to hay-making. I drove the rake which piled the swaths of timothy or clover in windrows and then, straddling the windrows, into rough cocks for the forks of the men who pitched and loaded them on hayracks. At the barn, I led the single horse which with a rope and pulleys could lift a quarter of a load at a time, draw it to the ridgepole, carry it spinning along the track, and, when the fork was tripped, drop the hay into the mow. Rain, of course, was always the hay-maker's risk and enemy, but in fine weather hay-making was the cleanest, sweetest work of the year.

After hay-making, threshing. No farm at Hope was large enough to need a threshing outfit of its own. A dozen or so farmers would organize a ring, hire a thresher, and arrange among themselves how many men and teams each farmer was to furnish and in what order they were to take their turns.

Our turn came. Chugging and coughing, a steam engine brought the high, huge, red threshing-machine along the road, made a wide turn at the lane gate, maneuvered its slow way to the place where the year's strawstack was to stand. There the engineer and his firemen pegged the thresher and the engine as far apart as the wide leather belt would reach. Men with teams and hayracks rattled to the field where the oats had already been cut and bound and set in shocks to dry. The first two hayracks loaded drew up alongside the thresher, another team backed a wagonbed under the spout out of which the threshed oats would pour, the feeder settled himself at the mouth of the machine with his cutters. With a hoot of the whistle the engine let loose its power till the thresher hummed. The men on the hayracks pitched sheaves upon the sloping tables on each side of the feeder, his helpers with quick knives cut the bands, and he with expert motions, now right hand now left, swept the sheaves headfirst into the humming throat, which growled as its iron teeth caught them. Then began a rhythmic thunder which stopped only at noon and night. A steady stream went as sheaves into the mouth, was broken up in those roaring bowels, and came out either as oats by the spout or as straw through the blower, which swung back and forth in an arc like the new moon.

This process was Hope's chief experience of what it means when machinery calls the dance and sets the pace. While the thresher ran, no man could step aside, and all men must work together. The loaded hayracks came, the unloaded hayracks went, without any interval. The knives of the cutters never rested and had always to be careful of the feeder's hands, which never rested except when one feeder spelled another. The stackers, working in the chaff with handkerchiefs around their necks and sometimes over their mouths, wallowed back and forth under the blower. The men or boys who waited at the spout kept shoveling the oats forward in their wagonbeds. Loaded, they started off for Fithian, eight miles away, urged their horses up the incline to the elevator, and saw their oats dumped into a bin which might be emptied that very day into a box-car going to Chicago. Then where? There was no philosopher in Hope to brood over the process, no poet to celebrate it, but it stirred us all by the loud noise and ruthless purpose which dominated us in our brief turn at tending the long line which at harvest reached from how many fields to how many mills, from seed in the ground to the nourished flesh of men and beasts.

Threshing was the large dramatic episode of our year, and after that the summer seemed to draw its breath. Old Settlers' Day, in August and at Potomac, never equaled the Fourth, lacking firecrackers and fireworks. The reminiscences of township pioneers, always old and seldom eloquent, could not rouse us as the Fourth's national patriotism had done. The wheel of the seasons turned quietly through burnt, brown, and yellow days into fall and the earliest crisp nights.

As my brothers and I went to school from the first of September to the first of June, I was a spectator not an actor in the main work of the farm during those months. Fall, winter, and spring meant to me, outside of school and play, only morning and evening chores: milking, lugging in fuel, running errands, helping my mother in the house. I remember little about cornhusking—shucking corn the farmers called it—except the sound of the men getting their horses out of the barn before daylight, the thud of ears thrown against the bumpboard, the ring of scoop-shovels as they unloaded at the corncrib. Corn-shelling was to threshing what Old Settlers' Day was to the Fourth of July—not unlike it, but a paler copy. About winter I remember best the horses, with shaggy coats, stamping in cold stalls, the cows shaking their stanchions and sending out vaporous breath, the sheep in their sheds crowding and snuffling and bleating—these and the English sparrows which fluttered in the lantern light when we went at night to stable or barn or shed, to kill the pests and save their heads for the bounty of two cents apiece which the township treasurer paid. I remember Christmas as a mysterious, spendthrift month, and do not remember Easter at all. The spring plowing comes back to me as the smell of straight furrows of black earth and the sight of birds following the plow to pick up worms and grubs. But once or twice in the spring, at sheep-shearing, I stayed out of school for a day or two, to tie up the fleeces as they came greasy and stinking from the shearing-floor, and to trample them into the enormous burlap bags in which they went off to the railroad and factory.

I appear to tell of one year though there were ten, and such different years as those I lived through when I was a small child and when I was as tall and almost as strong as any man. But one year was as much alike another as the seasons and the crops which in annual rotation ruled our lives. If we were never bored, however tired, it was because we were always busy. Remote from the world at large, we did not realize it. No radio and no movies let the world in upon us, and no telephone, till the last year, brought even our neighbors close. The automobile had not yet extended the radius of the farmer's life from four or five miles to forty or fifty. Except to go to school or church and to visit a few relatives, my brothers and I left the farm hardly a dozen times a year.

Our liveliest interruptions were the too rare visits of my mother's brothers. The twins, Uncle Warren and Uncle Wallace, went from college to be Columbian Guards at the World's Fair, and came back with fine tales. Then they had something—I never knew what—to do with railroads, and brought us news as rousing as if they had been sailors off at sea. Afterwards they followed our older Uncle Clinton and Uncle Mark to the Indian Territory, about which, when any of the four returned, we heard of Choctaws, Chickasaws, Creeks, Cherokees, Osages, railroads, ranches, hunting, cowboys, booms, and a coming country. Tall, lean, brown, bachelors and Democrats, smelling of strong tobacco, talking casually of towns and distances, they were like windows in our plain walls.

And there was reading. I can barely remember when I could not read, and except in the most crowded seasons I read hours a day. Few current books ever reached Hope. The first book I remember owning was Green's history of England, in five volumes, which I won as a prize at school when I was nine. Its chapters on the dim Anglo-Saxons stand up in my memory like old photographs. Hawthorne with his New England was less real, and Plutarch with his Greeks and Romans. We had the works of Scott, Dickens, Thackeray, Mark Twain. Like everybody else in Hope, we had Ben-Hur, which most people read as if it were part of the Apocrypha, and two or three volumes of James Whitcomb Riley, who belonged to Indiana but might have been writing about us. We had Gibbon, in whom I dipped. We had Shakespeare, whose poems I read before his plays, Oliver Wendell Holmes, whose humorous verses tickled my father to tears, and Whittier—but no Poe or Whitman, no Tennyson or Browning. I remember crying, at five or six, over the story of Evangeline, which my mother read me. When I was older I preferred the legends of Hiawatha, then the only mythology I knew. I read Fenimore Cooper and Irving, Pilgrim's Progress and Robinson Crusoe and Gulliver's Travels and the Last Days of Pompeii and Little Women and Quo Vadis? After I had discovered that I could order books by mail from Chicago, I bought books for all my birthday or Christmas presents to my family—always books I had not read myself. We all read.

We read greedily and uncritically. A book was a book, and it was interesting or it was not. We liked Dickens and Mark Twain best, and David Copperfield and Huckleberry Finn best of all. After my father's youngest brother committed suicide in Cincinnati, my brothers and I remembered that when, shortly before, he was staying with us he had read Huckleberry Finn and had not laughed once. We thought that this somehow explained the tragedy. If we had no new books to read, we read old ones again. From my father's medical books, which I read more than I let on, I learned a great deal about anatomy. I made little of the Compleat Angler, which my grandfather, angler himself, took for a kind of hand-book, though he often disagreed with it. He called Walton an old codger, but I doubt that he knew or cared when Walton lived. None of us knew or cared about literary chronology. Books for us were like stars, all apparently the same distance away, yet some brighter than others. Reading was simply experience otherwise denied us. We traveled without leaving Hope. When later we did leave, life was not so strange as we expected. Books had enlarged the village.

8

If, REMEMBERING, I make out life at Hope as a cool pastoral, I misrepresent it. There was the weather. Between its almost equatorial summers and its almost arctic winters Illinois has a range of temperature to be found in few quarters of the earth. In July or August the thermometer might stand for hours a day at 110 in the shade. After such days the sweltering nights of corn-growing weather brought no real relief. Men lay on top of unbearable sheets and horses sweat at midnight. It might be 30 below zero in January or February, when the cold came down like a clamp, and the roads froze in iron ruts. Such cold seldom lasted long, but was followed by sudden thaws, as trying as the next fierce spells of cold again. I wonder, now, at the fortitude with which we bore these extremes. It was the fortitude of ignorance. We barely knew that elsewhere the seasons could be easier. We no more thought of going south for the winter or north for the summer than if we were still in the eighteenth century, when the United States chose Washington to be its capital. Because we did not realize that we might suffer less from weather, we could not realize how much we suffered, and so perhaps suffered less.

After Spoon River became famous, my brother Mark once asked me if Hope, from which he went away at six, had been at all like that infested village. I recalled some dark or furtive story that I, still a boy, had picked up about every household in the neighborhood.

One Sunday night a farmer was murdered on his way

home from church—not our church, but the one just south of us. A scared rider came for my father, who the next morning brought fatal news. The farmer had quarreled with two of his hired men. They had armed themselves, waylaid him and his wife, and, when he whipped his team past them, had fired and killed him. The county sheriff arrested them and took them off to Danville, where they were hanged. We heard stories of their insolent bravado in the jail. One of them was said to wear a piece of rope around his neck, to toughen it. The other told a visitor that he had a new job for the fall: he was going to stretch hemp. In their native Kentucky they might have had ballads made and sung about them. Hope had no ballad-makers. The crime was remembered in prose.

Two farmers in Hope had a feud over a bad fence and roving stock. They did not speak when they met on the road, and usually avoided each other. But one day when one of them was in the blacksmith shop, the other came in, angry and vicious. Without a word he grabbed a spare wagon-spoke and attacked. The first, throwing up his arm, was struck with the end of the club on a fleshy muscle which tore like a rag. A great red-whiskered man, he came staggering and bawling to my father's office to have the ugly three-cornered tear sewed up. Nobody did anything about the assault. The victim was unpopular, the victor feared. That so small a man had won a fight and that so large a man had blubbered made the affair ridiculous.

Feuds, it is true, seldom lasted. They sank to grudges and died out, without actions to keep them alive. One of the farmers had a grudge against my father, because the farmer's son had died of some sickness which my father had been unable to cure. I heard only vaguely of the one-sided grudge, and never saw any outward signs of it. My grandfather, years before, had disputed with his nearest neighbor over the boundary line between their farms. Each of them had planted his hedge where he thought it ought to be, leaving a long strip of waste land which in time had grown up to a matted tangle of weeds and bushes. Called a devil's lane, it stood there as a stubborn memorial, meaning nothing. My grandfather and his neighbor, as old men, were civil enough, and one of the neighbor's daughters was my mother's closest friend. When, writing my first novel, I tried to work into it these two grudges, I found them the dry seed of a kind of drama alien to this community.

Violence at Hope was likely to be swift and savage. A furious man might beat a balky horse with a pitchfork or a trace-chain. Fathers might punish their sons with black-snake whips. There were brutal husbands, though public feeling was all against them, and if their wives left them, the wives got the sympathy. But interference in private matters came slowly if it ever came. Some of the farmhouses, we knew, were inviolate castles where evil things went on.

The scandals outnumbered the crimes and misdemeanors. A woman in the village, whose husband was a drover and often away from home, drifted into loose habits. Men visited her at night, and laughed about it at the village store. Whether or not she deserved her bad name from the first, she had it and was damned. The preacher one year set himself to save her, and he was damned too, and dismissed as certainly a fool and probably a lecher. Everyone talked, nobody told her husband. At last he found out when she had a child which he was sure could not be his. Divorced, she left for Danville to practice a trade. There she prospered, opened a disorderly house, and made her bad name conspicuous. For years she must have had a wider renown than any woman or man who had ever come from Hope.

Adultery in the village was so rare that I heard of no other instance of it, except that some of the rougher married men went disreputably to Danville. Circumstances at home made it almost impossible for a married woman ever to be alone with any man except her husband. On the prairie a call in the daytime was certain to be noticed, and the waking hours of the night were brief and domestic. Wives had few opportunities to stray, and, I think, fewer impulses. Married young, mothers soon, and generally overworked, they had neither strength nor leisure for adultery. I imagine that their sexual experience was curt and unimaginative. When they hinted at it, as they seldom did, they called it, revealingly, family duty. The married women fixed the sexual code of Hope, and the married men had to fall in with it. So did the unmarried women with respect to married men. Without women adultery could not thrive.

Fornication was not uncommon. Young men and women did their courting without chaperons, much of it in long drives on dark nights. When this led to hasty marriages and babies born six or seven months afterwards, it caused talk and reproach that gradually ceased if the offenders settled down and behaved themselves. Only the censorious and the humorous remembered such things long. Fornication that did not lead to marriage roused grave scandal. If a man seduced—ruined—a girl, and deserted her, her outraged father might drive her from the house. This seemed old-fashioned. In most cases she remained at home, outcast, till she married some other man who was not important enough to be fastidious. As she was punished more than her first lover, she was blamed more. "It's for the man to ask, and for the woman to say no," the blunt saying ran. The seducer's fault need not prevent his early marriage to some more prudent girl. Fornication at Hope, at least as I heard of it, was always serious or desperate with fear of conception, never light or merry. Women held to strict responsibility did not play at love.

The comedy of sex appeared in obscenity. On a farm like ours, even small boys could not overlook the hot deeds of potent rams, roosters, and gobblers, could not fail to get at the reason for them, and could not help making comparisons between them and human conduct. Boys of ten knew all that most of them would ever know about the theory and science of reproduction, and were more than ready for experience to teach them how to feel about it. Desire did not surprise them. They had gone to school in the barn. The barn was the men's house, where women seldom came, and where on rainy days the hired men joked. Mothers might speak of love as if it were always the sacred way to motherhood, and fathers as if it were a pleasing, harmless motive in the business of marriage. But there was still, boys knew, something unaccounted for: the rank impulse that rose in them like sap, salty and acute, agitating them. Into this the hired men, talking, let a crude light that seemed to answer morbid questions. When the hired men laughed, broad and lewd, the sultry air was stirred and the tension eased. Foul and false as it often was, their obscenity quieted while it excited us. It enlivened a passion which without them might have been too sentimental or too tragic. If obscenity was comedy, it was realism too.

The pioneer time had seen hard drinkers in Hope, but in the last years of the century liquor could not be bought within twenty miles and seldom reached us, though a few

men went on sprees to Danville. Gambling was heard of
only in men who speculated in grain on the Chicago Board
of Trade, and invariably lost their money. The other vices
of Hope were the greed which drove whole families to sense-
less toil, the avarice which denied them satisfactions they
might as well have had, the cruelty which came both from
anger and from stupidity. Hope was, I repeat, a microcosm.

9

OUR last night at Hope we spent not in the farmhouse but
in the village house where I had been born. The neighbors
who were our best friends had invited us there because our
own goods were packed and loaded, ready to leave at daylight. As I was to drive one of the wagons, I got up while it
was still dark, and walked across the fields to feed and harness my team.

Still dark, the night was beginning to break up. In the
close, high silence I could almost hear the rumble of the
dawn. The first birds fussed. Roosters crew. A dog barked.
Walking, I seemed to feel rather than see, over my shoulder, a faint light lessening the stars. I looked back and saw
the horizon pale and then flush. Thin rays from the sun
broke through and touched the sky above it. My mood rose
with the light, as if the sun were in me. I had been heavy
and relaxed with sleep, full of night. Walking alone between night and day, and both of them somehow inside me,
I expanded with a tingling, melting ecstasy, as if my bones
were water and my flesh were air. The earth under me, the

sky over me, had pulse and breath, and my own pulse and breath moved with them. I could hear my heart.

The horses were stirring in the barn, but the house was empty and quiet. I stopped for a moment and looked at them, at the cold white fences and the shadowy trees. There was no reflection in my mood, only boundless sensation. What I felt, now, was not the general night and day, earth and sky, but the farm itself, and the familiar ways of living there. On every rod of land I had worked or played, and I could have found my way blindfold anywhere. The farm was in me. I had eaten it as food. I had been sheltered by house and barn and tree, in every weather. The animals were hardly less kin to me than my family. My hands knew all the tools. If I had thought, I must have known that I was not merely leaving the farm but was being uprooted. Some of it would come with me. Some of me would stay behind. The filaments of habit and memory which bound me were tougher than I had ever realized. Even in my dissolving ecstasy I felt the pain of separation and half-foresaw a long homesickness.

The mood passed and left only my will, eager to go from the too-familiar farm and village to the unknown, promising town. I harnessed and hitched up the mules and waited for Guy to join me. Then we climbed on top of beds and chairs and tables for the slow, dusty drive.

BOOKS BY CARL VAN DOREN

AUTOBIOGRAPHY

Three Worlds

BIOGRAPHY

Benjamin Franklin
Thomas Love Peacock
James Branch Cabell
Swift
Sinclair Lewis

FICTION

Other Provinces
The Ninth Wave

LITERARY HISTORY AND CRITICISM

The American Novel
Contemporary American Novelists
The Roving Critic
Many Minds
American and British Literature since 1890
(*with Mark Van Doren*)
What Is American Literature?

EDITED

The Cambridge History of American Literature
Modern American Prose
An Anthology of World Prose